INTRODUCTION

Why did I write this book? Honestly on accident.

I sat down to write a letter. Old school, I know, but this was personal and needed to feel that way. This letter was to never make it to the receiver. This was a letter meant to be therapeutic for me and me alone. Something happened as I was writing, reliving and understanding the lessons learned, I thought that I wish someone had told me some of this earlier in life. It would have helped me out. So I decided to type it up and share just in case someone may need it. If I can touch one life with the lessons learned from mine, it will all have been worth the journey.

Thank you for taking time out to explore with me.

I ramble and I worry but the truth is that I am just an amazing woman who fell in love with an amazing woman. We had been magnets since we met 14 years ago. Constantly drawn to one another. For many years as friends only. Comfortable company. The thought is that I am the only person who really knows her. The truth is simply that I am the only person who ever SAW her. The real her. Her that she hides so well from the rest of the world and was too guarded to let others see. This is my blessing and my curse. I am excessively observant. A lot of women I have come across are far too self-obsessed to take the time and effort to truly see into someone else. They want all focus to remain on them but do not focus on themselves in the right ways. Men and women are both guilty of this. Some are conceited, some are so insecure that they use sex to get attention. Others, the social media junkies - are fake versions of themselves all for the "fans" on a webpage. I hope these lessons help you become your own biggest fan.

This is a story of lessons learned from REAL LIFE! The so called normal story of boy meets girl, girl falls in love, marriage, babies and happily ever after do not apply to this life I have lived. This is the REAL and RAW of it. I happened to do some of these things in chaotic order and some not at all.

For every man or woman left feeling like he/she isn't enough for someone

Broken hearted left a shell of someone

We are taught that love is something from a fairytale

So we don't understand how we can give it our all and it fail

It's true - it's not you or what you did or didn't do

It's not how hard you love, who the heart may choose

DEDICATION

To my dearest Chulo,

"I love you from a place where words are irrelevant."

These words will remain as the tattoo on your shoulder. Let it be a reminder that you have overcome every obstacle thrown in your way and you will always be a divine light to those around you. The ability to touch another human being in the ways you have touched my life is a gift. Never forget that you deserve all the love that comes your way.

I was fortunate to come across a woman that would change me forever. Thanks to you, these changes brought me the self-awareness to heal and to this day, I love you immensely.

I cannot thank enough for your support in allowing this story to be told. Your willingness to heal through this process is astounding.

Thank you!

THE LETTER

Dear you know who you are,

As I struggled to navigate the riddled sea of my emotions, I decided the best way to sift through my feelings is to do what I do best and write it out. Purge the feelings that have been playing out in my head in a whirlwind of confusion, lay it all out and sort through the wreckage. When you are feeling something deep inside and your first instinct is to push it deeper, tuck it away and stomp it down until you can no longer see any trace of it, it usually means that it is something that needs to be dealt with. Felt and dealt is what I like to call it. Feel everything, let it take over. If it is tears of pain, cry! You are allowed this. Bask in the memory, let it be. Then deal with it until you understand the feelings and where they are coming from. It is the only way to cleanse yourself. To cover yourself in the feelings and then wash them all away. We all need this. There are so many unspoken words that I have longed to relay. The first, of many, is that I unapologetically love, and I love you, so here goes...

I took a lot of time to reflect on how I could lose the person that I love most in the world. Not only lose them once but to lose them on multiple occasions was rough to handle. This is especially the case when the love is so strong. You can find yourself left with many nagging little questions: We all love questions. We have no problem asking many. It is why social media and "reality" TV is so constant and obsessive. Damn if we are not afraid of the answers though. We run from them. At times, we fabricate them and even will take it as far as to choose to ignore or flat out refuse to believe the answers we are given. The truth is that I was terrified so I just dove in.

What does this mean for my future? I find that we spend so much time creating a plan and very little time on the execution of said plan. My advice: do not try to plan your future as it will only lead you down a frustrating path heavy with feelings of failure. Contrary to what we like to believe, every plan can fail and failure is just an accomplishment that you were not aware of. How do you end the comparison game that we like to play? Just don't do it. When you notice that you are picking away at someone when they do things differently than another, step away from it and give them a clean slate. They have no idea what another may have brought to you before them. They are only attempting to give you what they are and what they have. What am I even looking for at this point? We all know that when you look for specificity, you will NOT find it but when you open up to new things, you will find them all around you. Remember that you attract what you put out.

Then come some of the bigger questions that we continuously ask ourselves yet never truly answer for the fear of having to face those answers. Teach yourself to do the opposite. Search for the answers and it will change your life. I promise! This will cause you to dig into yourself. We avoid doing the work we need to on ourselves at times by latching onto the concerns and baggage of others. Helping all those that we can and hoping to help even those that we cannot all in an attempt to avoid unpacking the answers to each and every question, digging deep enough to face them, especially the cold and ugly ones.

Do I settle for a happiness that is less than? To a certain degree, yes. I had to learn to accept the fact that I will not be able to achieve the same level of happiness I once had but that happiness was still a possibility. A new and different way to feel it. A different person to earn it. That old touch and feel and scent, I will still yearn it. The candle may have flickered out but I am so glad we burned it. This is what I was feeling. I had to learn how to be happy without the presence of someone who had been so much to my life. I had to know for myself that this was a possibility so I set out to find my new happy.

We as humans find it easier to question others and rarely put ourselves under the microscope when this is where the magic can happen. Do I sit back and be alone? There will always be a sense of loneliness in every person who has lost love. It does not mean that you give up on finding love altogether, just that you may have to work harder to bring it to fruition in your life. Stop yourself from looking for that same thing you had because you cannot replicate it. You should not want to. It is an involuntary thing to automatically want to find what you have lost. The true treasure is to realize that when you lose something or someone, they are not gone per se. Placed somewhere outside the physical reach of your ill perceived perception of possession, yes. It may stay where it lay or someone else may find and claim as their own. When they find it, rest assured that it is no longer the same thing that you have lost. It has changed with the time you have spent apart causing a shift–whether you think it is significant or not. The butterfly effect, if you will. It only takes one second, one touch or one moment to change an entire course for each of us. When someone else gains possession and you are still longing for the possession you once had, understand this: You two are fighting for two different people so you should hold it tight and relish in the memories you have of what you once had.

These were the top questions I had for myself; will I ever give 100% of myself again? This one I struggle with due to the fact that I have not yet returned to my 100% self, therefore I do not have it to give to another. Will I find 100% of myself again? This is the real question. My percentage ranges from about 70-85 depending on the day but I am hopeful. Then begs the question, is that enough for another human being looking for love, looking for more? This is not for you to figure out. It is up to the other people who come into your life. Do not convince yourself that it will be unfair to ask anyone to accept you or what you have to offer. As you develop relationships, share your truths, and let them make the educated decision for themselves. People will do what they want to in the end.

It would seem for once as though my tendency to over-analyze may come in handy with this process. This reflection of feelings had me in a tailspin for quite some time but I must say that I came out of it with great lessons. These lessons I decided to share in hopes that more of us could learn from them. Lessons that you inadvertently taught me and I am thankful for now.

Is it ME?

I am left alone and I don't like it

It is a lot to face me when I can no longer recognize it

The reflection is a shell, empty, spent

How do I begin to work the puzzle of pieces I am in?

I find one and place it next to another

These shards do not fit into each other

This continues until I am overwhelmed, smothered

Unaware of all this journey will lead me to discover

With patience I come together piece by piece

Slowly feeling the pain decrease

I will somehow miss the ache, the release

As I finger the scars that left me creased

Is it me? The forever girl no one wants to keep?

The one they run from when it gets too deep?

The one you call for even in sleep?

Is it my sows that you are afraid to reap?

Alone again, no one ready for me

A taunting game to pull me close, a plaything

Yet loyalty grows for those less deserving

I cut my teeth on the bitterness they feed me

What is wrong with the way I love?

No one can reciprocate, it's too much

Am I wrong that I can isolate my craving to just one touch?

Others need more or is this just a crutch

In and out of my life like this is double dutch

Scared to make the choice which one

In or out - let it be done, I cannot keep up

Is it me, alone again when I wake up?

HEALING

Originally, I only saw the fault and flaws in me because that is naturally my default stance. I found myself constantly trying to find answers to detrimental questions like, "What is wrong with me? Why am I never enough?" If you find yourself doing this, STOP! Backtrack a bit and take a minute to coach yourself in another direction. It is never about what is wrong with you! This is only a sign that along the way, life has made you doubt yourself, to second guess yourself and who you are. We do not begin life unsure of ourselves, feeling "less than," or "not good enough." Somewhere along the road we have traveled, someone threw a speed-bump in your path causing you to slow down or to fall altogether. As we slow our course due to the obstacles placed by others, we stumble because we are trying so hard to see the view that they see. We then adopt the perception of others. We start to see ourselves through their eyes and eventually, begin to believe their perception. We begin to intercept our self-esteem with the twisted visions of what other people think or say. We give away our power to other people whether we mean to or not. The only way to maintain self is to keep your self-esteem intact. Love yourself in the way you want others to or they will struggle to love you also. Don't and it will only chip away at the confidence that you started with. See, it does not matter whether that speed-bump was a rejection, an insult, or a perception that holds no truth. The damage at that point is done. The soft spot where it hit you has now hardened and we continue to harden with each blow. We have taken whatever caused that bump in the road and put it in our mental storage and we carry it with us into and through adulthood where we will only gain more bumps and bruises. Unfortunately, others suffer from the hardness brought on by the people that have come into our lives previously. It is up to us to gain the self-awareness needed in order to mitigate these situations.

When things go bad in any relationship, we all want to be in a position to say that it is NOT me, to say that it is the fault of the other party in all aspects, but this is not reality. I would later come to understand that it is both. I believe both. Fault will almost always lie with both parties. There are no innocents in this aspect. Do not waste time trying to make it so. We all have our parts to own. Some big and some small. Everything is circumstantial. I always saw you as being flawed in the most beautiful way but could not allow myself to feel the same for me. Me, I was much harder on as we often are by nature as we expect so much more from ourselves than we do others. We then learn to place those expectations onto others. Yep, I said it. Read it again if you need to. A lot of the expectations we push onto others stem from those we have of ourselves. Think about it!

We are under the assumption that we know ourselves better than anyone ever could but remember those speedbumps that we've encountered? Those perceptions of others that we come to believe as truth? At times, getting lost in the land of everyone else hinders us from learning who we really are.

I believe, now, that I am an amazing woman in so many ways and for many different reasons. I also believe the same about you. I could not wrap my head around how we could not show up in this form for each other??? This was the thought that brought me pause and began this letter. It is not correct or fair to assume now that we did not present our best selves to one another when we had many beautiful years of just that.

Music!!! It literally makes up most of the great memories. We have spent many nights just vibing to music and talking until the sun came up. Music transcends. It can take you back to a place or time without pretense. I have vivid memories of our house with our friends and family. Listening to the new Keri Hilson, Ledisi, or Day26 albums and having our own private concerts, Sunday morning gospel cleaning sessions always makes me think about the boys upset that I woke them up to it or just surrendering and singing along with us cause they knew it was time to get up. Those faces and those times make it all so worth it. So much music that brings me back to happy times.

That song that comes on randomly as you clean the house and it stops you, puts you in a different space and time. The one that brings back the sensations of a touch or a kiss. The ones that hold so many emotions of happiness, anger, or ecstasy. It all comes rushing through you and you have no control of it. The songs that we have all skipped or turned off cause we were not ready to go there mentally? I chose to finally feel all of it. This is the only way to change or to grow. I no longer turned off songs that made me think of you. I sang them, danced to them, spoke to you through them. I felt you in ways that I missed, in pain that I was relieved from, in longing for the gentle caresses, the simple eye squints that made my knees weak. All of it was as it should be, an emotional roller coaster that left my head spinning. I loved every minute of it...it was intoxicating. You and I dancing in the kitchen with Chris Brown and Keri Hilson singing "Superhuman" in the background, staring into the each other's eyes, singing in each other's faces and feeling so safe. Sharing our long held secrets with one another. Even now, these memories feel like home. I can even smell the incense burning in the air.

Waking up with the house full of the people we love after a long night out to find that no one can leave as it decided to snow an unbelievable amount while we slept. We were in our bubble. We spent a few days snowed-in cooking and laughing. Singing and dancing. The boys, not even the kids, but the adult boys building a snowman and naming it Sasha Frost as Beyonce's Sasha fierce album was big in the minds of all of the creatives in the house. That first morning as everyone was calling into work to check on the status of it all and calling family members to make sure everyone was safe, there was a palpable excitement in knowing that we were about to have the best time ever! There was no better residence to be snowed in on that day.

Munchies had a full snack drawer we kept for him in the kitchen so he could not have been happier, Superstar who loved everything we cooked was just excited to chill, cook and eat at the house. Brother, who had moved in long before this, was happy that he had his boo there and they were snowed in with us. We were with some of our constants. We were good. So much fun to be had. The memory of Superstar singing Whitney Houston's "I wanna dance with somebody" as he cuddled on the couch and then irritated at the one note cadence of Karyn White "superwoman" still makes me smile. Munchies dancing on the kitchen counter with the strobe light we borrowed from the neighbors. The best!

Kidnapping the little brother on his birthday, blindfolded and all. We took him to see the play Chicago in Seattle and enjoyed every minute of it. Then took him driving around the city all the while our friends were setting up the house where a surprise party was waiting. It was a blast. Any time I can do something to show appreciation for people in my life, it is a positive.

Our sons lighting up in the kitchen when we made homemade pizzas for dinner. The smiles on their faces when they accomplished this small task was unforgettable. The new tradition was created! Them arguing about what to watch and who was better at what, then turning around and sticking up for one another. True brothers. We created this family and these bonds cannot be broken no matter how much time and distance are put in the way.

Christmas has always easily been my favorite holiday. Every year, I would plan a holiday party where we could all do things we would never do otherwise. We made paper snowflakes one year and hung them from the ceiling and it made the holidays so apparent. Decorating sugar cookies and voting on the best decorations (most of which were eaten before we could get the pictures taken) people lit up like little kids cause this is a part of the brain that as adults, we rarely get to use. Baking with you in the kitchen for hours was always so therapeutic for me as I had never before enjoyed sharing the kitchen with anyone. I laugh to myself about this. In all things we did there was a synchronicity that was always prevalent. There were no negative memories of these times.

This is where my healing needed to take place.

The tendency to get stuck on the negative is only an attempt to heal. I hate to be the one to break it to you but this is a band aid for healing at best. Allowing negative things to spiral instead of dropping it down the drain will not heal the wounds, only cover them temporarily slowing the bleeding. A mask of sorts. This will allow you to hide the bruises but they will reappear when you do not acknowledge the source of your pain. We have to learn to talk about the happy. We are silent when things are good and then have this urge to vent out the bad, when things are going wrong. STOP. DOING. THAT. Imagine life if we all vented out the good—the positive, the things we love and the joy that people bring to our lives. What would that kind of life look like for you? The outlook is so much more appealing, isn't it?

I challenge all who have had a recent or even not so recent break-up to stop saying negative things about this person and focus on what made you happy in the relationship. I urge you to stop rattling off solely their list of cons. Remember there were good times. What was it that made you fall to begin with? I know it is against our nature, but this train of thought allows you to see this person in the light that made you love. You were in the relationship for a reason. Go to that place and heal from love. Let the love inside of you swell with each positive memory. Think about what lessons you can take away from having had this experience in your life. Unpack anything that comes up in the process. This is the healthiest space to begin to heal from as it will thoroughly clean all wounds, stitch you up and initiate proper healing.

With you, I never sponsored. I never had to. We built first a friendship that was solid on truth. You know things about me that no one else ever will. I was so soft with you—going against my own natural instinct. I was raw and open and completely vulnerable, allowing you to know me in ways no one ever truly had... It scared me more than anything I had ever felt. It didn't matter. This was IT for me. You were IT, for me. I gave my heart willingly, yet without choice and I trusted you with it. I had never before done that. Trusted that way. I had already grown this trust through our friendship so making the transition to lovers was so seamless that it had happened before I was done convincing myself that it was okay. I was completely undone. Like a pretty purple bow tied on top of a gift, one touch and I'd quickly release every loop and leave the gift wide open for you. Fears are detrimental as they are usually involuntary. Me with you: You reached every soft spot that I had left along with a few that I was unaware of. With the intensity of that vulnerability comes a lot of fear. To put it in perspective, and I cannot speak for you, but that fear, for me, at times, was crippling. Fear can cause each of us to talk differently and behave strangely and to possibly stop doing the things that come naturally for us and instead begin acting under the pretense of what we think someone else wants while ignoring our ignorance to the fact that we have no idea.

I believe that this is where sponsors are born. The dating process, for instance, finds itself full of sponsorship. You want someone to like you so you show them what they want to see. We give them what they like, forgetting about what we like as well as who we actually are. We become great actors portraying a character Academy Award-worthy that was built on the false information we gathered. We create relationships built on fantasy, which is the reason most do not make it through the phase of the relationship when the honeymoon is over and reality sets in. When they have to deal with finding out that the person they spent their time falling for doesn't actually exist entirely. They can only know the abbreviated version of this person. A representative of who this person truly is. One of my favorite personalities Dr. Chris Donoghue, PhD, LCSW, CST, ACS says, "date to be known, not to be liked." I believe that this is sound advice. If you display your true self, you then can gauge the true compatibility between you and another.

I have been extremely lucky in my dating life, barely requiring one at all. I have only dated maybe one person that I had not previously known. I like to know the foundation of a person prior to beginning anything. I like to know the core values and morals. I also like having the time to see the mask fall. The one that they hide behind until the comfort sets in. I think that my younger self thought this was a way to play it safe yet it seemed to be a severely flawed tactic as I have yet to maintain my own safety or that of my heart. I am not one for small talk and getting to know you only to find out later that I am uninterested has always seemed like a waste of time to me. Another lesson learned: time is never wasted unless you learn nothing from it.

FEAR

As I pulled back the years and took a closer look, I can clearly see the turning point. The exact moment when something shifted and it all comes down to the fears we have had:

To show your perspective I will share our words.

Words from me: Tue 10/6/2009 10:41 AM

Feel like I have shattered in pieces when you tell me you are not sure of this commitment though I know you have your reasons. I feel as if I exposed all flesh and bone to you because my safety with you I believed was true. Your doubts have whipped me with a cat of nine tails and all I can do is let out the wails. Help me don't hurt me, love me don't leave me, I am all yours though the complications deceive me...and you. I am yours for the taking and maybe I am mistaking but you seem to want to shove me away. I hold on to you tighter cause it is like gasoline and a lighter, I can tell you want to run, yet you haven't heard the gun so why do you fight it? The flames have ignited and you let it burn as the fear consumes your mind. Why can't you see that this is our time? There will be no other and you may wake only to discover we are gone. We naturally are like a perfect lyric over a tight beat you and me. Outside noises muffle our melody and only when we clear them will you begin to hear it.

-Lyric

Words from you: Tue 10/6/2009, 11:53 AM

Baby,

Honestly - I get caught up in my fears too, and start feeling like I'm suffocating and can't breathe - like my freedom was just flushed down the toilet...is this really going to work? Does she really trust me? - but when I slap myself I shake out of it and say...chill out - you have so much love & joy with her, peace, comfort, admiration.... She's beautiful, intelligent - sexy, creative, tolerant, funny..... so yes I get wrapped up in my own fears and BS but bottom line - we are bonnie and Clyde... us together, forever... Xnlyric4eva

- snap out of it

I love you, from the depths of my soul and as hard as I know how to love.... X

Notice how fear can lead you down a never ending path of thinking you know what is going on in someone else's thoughts? Stop trying to read minds. I am extremely guilty of this. I get lost between over-analyzing and assuming—neither of which is a great place to be. Part of this comes from paranoia brought on, again, by others that have laid speed-bumps in your path. Let people tell you what they want and then, allow them show you. If the two begin to contradict, only then is it time to re-evaluate the plan. Have a quick recap, check the temperature and move forward from there. We sometimes think we know what we want only to find that we were wrong. Allow humans to human. We grow and change at a rapid pace so it is natural to see how our wants could do the same. This is why it is imperative to know the core values of a person. These are deeply rooted and seldom change.

The problems, I now see came long before the destruction…

As I sat with you on a night many years ago, we discussed my feelings for another. I was unsure and planning a trip to figure it all out. A trip to see this person. It's a bitch what hindsight will allow you to see cause though your words were supportive and curious, your eyes were pleading and hoping. I can see the expression on your face so clearly now that it hurts me to remember it cause how could I have missed it? This is it! This is where I broke it. Where the first tear in the fabric of us and of our trust was inflicted!

Though I know now how, what I thought was being in love with two people, was obviously more my fear of abandonment, of being alone. You gave me that moment to assure you. That one moment to keep you, to hold on to us, to show you that I would not abandon you and I failed miserably. If time travel were ever to be a possibility, I know now that this is the moment I would return to, change my number and end all communication because I will understand that there was always only you.

I was simply afraid! I let this fear guide me, ignoring reason, my heart, and my mind. This was the kind of fear that embedded itself and became hard to shake. It all stems from a kiss. A kiss that you shared with another had lead me in a tumultuous direction. I was headed toward something I was always better without. There are these small betrayals in the beginning of relationships that we sometimes gloss over without ever actually addressing.

Why do we wait for the end of a relationship to seek closure when we should do the work to ensure the closure of these tiny wounds and red flags that add to the bloodshed later? They are not insignificant. If you close these along the way, you will end nothing with open wounds. Close them when they happen, do not bite your tongue to keep the peace, do not pretend to forgive when you are in pain! The phrase "Every little bit hurts," came from somewhere.

See how not truly knowing yourself coupled with fear can blind you from the affect it is having on your partner? I will say that though I thought I already knew all of my flaws, I was wrong. You must allow your relationships, past and present to teach you about yourself as much as they teach you about who you are with. We oftentimes focus so hard on another that we forget to take care of our own needs and this is where people end up lost. We spend so much of our lives studying others, wanting to know everything about them, and we stop trying to learn about ourselves. You are the only person that you have to face in the mirror every day of your life. You should know most about you. How can you truly allow someone to know you if you don't take the time to know yourself first? This, too, can lead to sponsorship. You do not need to do that. You simply need to know who you are and share it until you find that person that can both enhance and embrace it all.

That is why we do not like to hear what others have to say about us. We call it projection when oftentimes it is not. It is just a reminder of a speed-bump that you do not want to return to. It is a trigger that causes you to mentally time travel backward to a painful memory or emotion, so we reject it in any way we can. I am not insisting that we relive our traumas but that we reflect on them solely in order to learn from them. Instead of instantly adopting the perception of another, aim to understand the perception. Take it apart and find out what about it is true and what is not because you, at that point, have most likely stopped paying attention to yourself and could learn something new. Never stop learning about yourself and never stunt your growth for anyone. If you find yourself in a situation where someone berates you for changing, throwing it as an insult that you have changed, tell them thank you and you're welcome. It is a compliment no matter how it was intended. If you are not changing, you are not growing. The ideal is to be with someone that will push you to grow and to do so together.

Grow. Change. Do it together and remember to congratulate each other on the strides you make no matter how small.

We are very much alike, you and I. Hard to believe but so true. I wonder if that is where the ease of understanding each other comes from. The mental stimulation and the effortless conversation. The defense mechanisms, the runner syndrome. We both have these embedded in our psyche due to our pasts. They say that most of what makes us happens early in childhood-scars that have never healed. Most, never addressed or even spoken aloud. Some we unsuccessfully attempt to forget and others we cannot even recall because the human condition blocks it away behind a brick wall for our own protection. That is the theory. Protection. These walls can also lead to the comfort of isolation. This can be our demise in any relationship situation as we cannot reflect in order to dissect and heal properly. You made me want to heal for the first time. I wanted to stop treading water and swim through the rough waters until we found the boat that would carry us to shore.

So, needless to say, I took that trip – leaving behind what I truly wanted. For what? To see if, by chance, I wanted something else? WTF was I thinking? I will tell you in full transparency that I was thinking as I often do: in self-sabotage mode. That this was too good to be true. That maybe all those speed-bumps along the way telling me that you could never love me that way, were legit. I was thinking that this was a somehow sordid way to protect my heart, when I should have been protecting yours. I also, in my young mind, wanted to know if you'd fight for me. Ugh! Young and dumb. For some unknown reason, that meant something to me. It was a sign of love? A statement that I meant something to you and was worth fighting for. In that young mind, I expected you to fight for me as I walked away from you? Something in my twisted mind made this make sense at the time. This was, by far, my first, and worst, offense.

From this moment when I popped the bubble that we were in, I lost you. You stopped trusting me with your heart and began to build a suit of armor for your own protection. Protection from me; the person who you could no longer tell loved you such an insane amount. With that suit came distance. At the time, I could not understand or see why this was happening. It would later make perfect sense. When it no longer matters, yes, yet I am enamored with the clarity of it now. So naive that I could think that our love would heal the hurt that I caused. That all would be okay cause what we had, would carry us through. That we were unbreakable. Love is never enough to carry a relationship as relationships are made up of so many things other than the love.

I spent a lot of years trying to make this horrible mistake right. Years trying to prove to you what your heart could no longer allow me to do. To have and protect it. You, I believe also spent years attempting to allow me this privilege, striving to allow me to show you this but you could not as you no longer trusted me with you, your heart, or the protection of either. You believed that you were giving me chances, only, you were already gone. It was all under false pretense. You wanted me but also wanted to make sure that you did not feel that hurt again. In doing so, you formed a lineup, a bumper, just in case I hit you with it again. This bumper made you feel like you had a backup plan if ever I tried to hurt you again. They would soften the blow. They were somewhere safe to land because you would not give them the power you had given me. The power to cause you pain. Love is power.

The Two of US

I can try to explain it but no one will get it but us

That I can feel your presence from a mile away deep in my
gut

So many things happen in my body before my eyes see

Before our lips speak

Body tingles, light sweat, anticipation on the tips of my
nerves

Butterflies at the thought of your hands on my curves

I am aware of you at all times in my proximity

The air is penetrated by the connectivity

It is unfair for those that surround us to witness, I accept this

Yet it is something like a drug and I cannot make excuses for
what is infinite

The perception has always been on the tips of tongues as real
love

Something unspoken but felt by those around us

Date: Thu, 31 Jul 2014 07:07:24 -0700

Subject: You

From: lyric

To: X

I have to say to you that I am deeply in love with everything that is us. I thank you for last night. I'm so glad you allow me to be the person you cry with, get angry with, parent with...talk, laugh, and debate with. I did the best I could to just hold you and let you know I am here. I was so glad to see your happy face this morning. Smiling and loving. Made me giddy. Yesterday is done and here you are. You are refreshed and cleansed. Have a fabulous day my gorgeous boi. - Lyric

On Jul 31, 2014 7:22 AM, "X" wrote:

I know I could have survived those moments last night without you - the ahhh ha was, I don't ever want to. You complete and complement everything I am. I'm entirely thankful and humbled by the fact I wake up each morning to see you and love you all over again. We were created to do, exactly what we're doing.... together.

I love you with everything I am. X

On Thu, Jul 31, 2014, 07:41 lyric wrote:

I'm all about that. Muah!

SOULMATES

Soulmate: A person with whom one has a strong affinity, shared values and tastes, and often a romantic bond.

It has been said that there is a soulmate out there for everyone. Though a soulmate usually breeds the thought of significant romantic relationships in which you share something truly unique, I dare to stretch this definition to mean much more. That a soulmate can come in many different ways. It can be a friend that you are bonded to. You may speak seldom, though when you do, it seems as no time has passed at all. A friend that will always remain a constant in your life. Your person! The one that you want to call first when BIG things happen in your life or when you eat something delicious and know they would enjoy it. The person that you can tell all of your secrets and they will not judge you or repeat it to another. Then, there is the more common meaning; of a love that can never be matched. A passion that can never be replicated. The love of your soul, not just your life. The one you feel lucky to have and in many cases grieve that you've lost. My soul sings at the thought of you, my body alerts me to your presence before my eyes can confirm it—kind of love. This is what we had.

I expected with distance and time that all of this would all change. That one day we would see each other and I'd feel nothing aside from how nice to see an old friend. I may never know if this is even humanly possible for me but even if these changes never happen, I am okay with it as it is a reminder that I am one of the lucky ones to have ever had a one of a kind love like that.

I believe that "getting over" a person is something that we say to appease others. That if you truly love another person on a soul level, you always will at least in some regard. If you find yourself feeling nothing for them at all, you most likely never fell completely in love with them and it was more so the idea of them or the potential in them that you loved. Not the reality. We often confuse the two. Sometimes we just fall in love with the idea of love. What we have been taught is love is vastly different from what love really is. It benefits us to know the difference. To know if we are in love with the person in front of us or simply in love with the fact that they love us. At times people stay with people for the way the other party feels for them even if it is not reciprocated. This is another instance of not pleasing ourselves internally but pacifying someone else for fear of hurting them. We are doing the opposite of what the intention is as they should be with someone that will feel the same way about them and you are hindering them from that. Let them go.

I have always loved hard and completely. Being with you taught me what this really means. Prior to that, I was loving all the wrong people and staying for all the wrong reasons. I have heard from far too many people about how I need to "get over" you, get over the things people have done to me or people in general.

Note to all: Stop telling people WHAT or WHO they should get over. No one knows how another is affected by these words. It implies that they are in a sad state, almost that they need help due to the fact that they are moving at a rate too slow compared to others. This is asking people to be compliant with social norms. No thank you!

In reality, they are being honest where others choose to lie saying that they are "over" a person only to see them out with someone else and find themselves drunk and crying in a bathroom stall somewhere.

You do not have to "get over" but you must get through. If you could grow and push through the loss and the pain, you can begin to work through it. Over is finite (we as humans are not). Through is where you want to be, pushing through the sad days and being happy day by day. You are allowed to love people through it all. The pain, the hurt, the loneliness, the tears, and all the destruction. DO NOT apologize for it, embrace it. This is a positive path on a long journey of self-allowance. We feel things for a reason, do not ignore these things. It is your bodies' way of telling you to learn or grow from it.

 I knew for sure that I loved you completely when was told that you were uninhibitedly happy with another and my soul was shining for you. It was so nice to see you fulfilled. To (truly) love someone is to honestly wish them nothing but happiness, whether that happiness includes you or not. To want for them to find what they were missing and love it for them. To fade to the back and wish them well no matter how much it hurts to miss them. To NOT pick up the phone when all you want to do is hear their voice, to say Happy Birthday or Merry Christmas? To NOT say anything at all. This is love.

It also made me look back at those who claimed to love me but could not find it in their hearts to ever be happy for me in times when I found myself so. Those who try to make you believe that no one can love you like them are simply implying that you should settle for them cause you cannot find better. This is not love and these words will never be true. This comes from fear also. If you find yourself with someone who claims these things, challenge it. Ask them why? If they can feel it for you, why couldn't another? Then ask them what it is that they are afraid of that would cause them to say such an insecure and hurtful statement. We all can have the love we want if we can heal from the speed bumps and be patient. Nothing worth having comes without hard work and patience.

IF you harbor ill feelings for a person or wish them unwell cause they hurt you or left you, that is not love. Chances are that you have hurt them at some point also. Relationships are pain. They are full of pushing and pulling, fighting and making up, debates and misunderstandings. You have found your life partner when you can pull and push each other in many directions, and decide when you need to push together to get over the speedbumps that you threw down at each other in the heat of the moment. A common side effect of relationships is knowing your partner so well that your tongue becomes the weapon of choice. You know what is going to push the right buttons and how to activate the wrong ones. These are the speedbumps we give each other in the middle of an argument. Those that we forgive at the end of it and bring back up later. You cannot forgive something but continue to bring it back into the relationship. You may lay it at their feet and see what they do with it. If you then remain, you have to let that be. Love it or leave it alone. The ammunition of miscommunication. If this is where you are and you cannot be happy for their happy, you may not have loved them at all, you just wanted them. Possibly, you do not even want them but simply want no one else to have them. This is usually cause you have put in your time and work attempting to help them grow. Of course you want to reap the benefits but in truth this is Selfish! There is always the chance that they grow into someone who will surpass you. We all want things but do we need them? To love is to need. To feel incomplete and empty without it. You want the cute shoes in the store window but do you need them? You need your next meal for sustenance. Loving someone entirely means that they are that meal. You need them the same way. The hunger pangs you feel in your stomach reminding you that you need food? With love, it is a pang in your heart for that space to be filled that can only be filled by that one person.

Others can fill many other spaces and occupy time and still, only this person can occupy your thoughts, your mind, and your spirit. This is an invasion that you are helpless to stop. A love that most never feel, see, or touch. The love made up of movies and books that you now roll your eyes at cause you do not believe it can end well. It is almost purposely branded as a fantasy. Unattainable.

It exists!

It may not come riding up on a horse and carriage or serenading you to a catchy melody but it can come in many other ways. You must stay open to the possibility that it will not look the way you have imagined.

I would almost venture to say that a lot of us have feasted on it but only as an appetizer. Smelled and were enticed. Touched and were curious. Tasted and enjoyed, all without knowing what you were sampling. Then, moving on to something else that presents as more filling. In reminiscence, if you had taken the time to enjoy and experience that small bite, you could have been full for life. Damn hindsight!

I came back from this trip and you took me. I may never know why. Perhaps you too, thought that we would be okay. That now this chapter was closed and we can begin again? Maybe you thought that you could allow me again to be the holder of your heart? This was not the case at all.

Loves' Walk

Love is a long walk in the blistering cold

It will conform to your body and hold you close

It is an addictive drug and can lead to overdose

And when it is real, it will consume you

It will forget all reason and assume you

Have to have it

It is a swim against the current

Nothing will deter it

Soft as a whisper and loud as the bass drum

Spins you like the salsa and leaves a sweet taste on the
tongue

Love is joy laced with pain

Love is giving power you can never regain

It is not all roses and candy canes

It is a high speed chase changing lanes

Love is all you want it to be

Until it is not and we vow to stay free

No longer wanting to swim in it

Still we test the waters with a toe dip

Next thing you know drowning, can't breathe

Until you can

And never again want to touch sand

Love is a storming sea that lulls you to sleep

Waking up from it feels like defeat

Love is dependent on the warmth of your body heat

Love is patient and love is kind

Love is the highest state of mind

ENTRANCE OF OTHERS

This decline happened fast and hard. Again, this is all my perception. It seemed as if there was a physical need to hurt me back after this trip. That for some reason, you could not be with just me. You required the attention and maybe, safety of others. It is very well possible that this was always the case but the honeymoon hype held your attention for a bit and lasted longer than usual. The timing could have been a coincidence but I am still on the fence as to if I believe in them at all. I will always wonder if this was a consequence of my actions and your poor decisions or if it was inevitable. Was it always there waiting in the shadows?

The first transgression was easy to forgive since I felt that I deserved it at that point. The guilt was weighing on me. Wrong again – no one, not one single human being, deserves to be hurt by another. Two wrongs will never make a right and in order to take care of each other (which is what we need more of on this planet) we must learn to take care of others. Especially those we claim to love.

Instincts are the flame of many forest fires. When you feel something inside, not only ask the tough questions, answer them, knowing the answer may be your worst fear. When your gut is telling you something is off, when your partner lies it off and tells you that you are just insecure and creating things in your head that are not there, this too, can chip away at one's self confidence.

While planning a surprise birthday party to honor you and all that you mean to not only me but my family as well as our friends, I watched this come to fruition. After months of hearing that I was just insecure and making up things that were not there. Celebration underway, while in the kitchen, I glanced over to see the eye contact between the two of you and my heart falls into my feet. The party was over for me and I could conjure up nothing but tears. I tried to stop them but they were unending. As I lay in our bed horrified and embarrassed all at the same time, the party goes on for you. To this day, I cannot forget this feeling. With all the pain I had undergone with others preceding her, I had been, dare I say, lucky to have never seen it with my own eyes. I had always assumed that the others meant less. Less than me. We do that, convince ourselves that we are the exceptions. I believed that you saved your heart and your love for me. Your passion was undeniable and I should have known that you would be helpless to hold back the overflow no matter who was allowed to indulge. It was not just for me, it was a part of you that many would experience. I still find myself hoping that there was a part, no matter how big or how small, one piece that was just ours. That no one else could come close to. One piece that you reserved for only me as I had for you.

The lesson hidden inside all the pain is simple. Trust yourself more. Trust that if anyone can protect you, it IS you and you alone. Instincts are there for a reason. They alert us when something is not right. DO NOT ignore this. You are created to feel and to love. When those sick feelings sit in the pit of your stomach alerting you, pay attention and address them.

Do not let anyone blow them off when you need answers. These answers are your education and you cannot make an informed decision without them as to what direction you would like to go. You need to know where you stand in the priority list and make sure that you are always number one on your own list. Lastly, remember that if you have to go and ask someone else's opinion, you most likely already know the answer. Validate yourself. Do not look to others to do it for you.

The ME now is a changed person in that aspect. Knowing the difference between plain insecurities and instincts can save a lot of pain later on. This particular pain became ever-present for me. The faces changed, the story didn't. It is funny to me now because you always claimed I was playing victim when I actually felt like I deserved it – at least for a while. Let me be clear now–I know that I did not deserve any of it! What was not properly conveyed on my part is that I stayed more so because I viewed you as the victim of my stupidity and thought I was laying in the bed I made for myself. Neither of us were happy and the recipe was disastrous. This became our lives and I still stood strong. Why? Why did I take on the role of a housewife without a partner?

You thought I was there for convenience and I allowed you to think it cause I lacked the energy to try to get you to understand that I was there for presence, my energy was spent. I was there thinking that one day, you would look at me the way you used to. You would realize that I was what you wanted and I had finally proven my loyalty to you by not leaving, taking care to cater to the abandonment issues that we both come with. I truly believed that you were testing me to see if I would abandon you again when you did something that hurt me. Would I run at the first sign of pain? Clearly not the case but I was there thinking that all would be well if I was just patient. You would see that I could love you through it all. I could prove it to you if I was just patient. There is a point where patience becomes complacency. A point where this pain becomes self –inflicted. When I lay next to you listening to your laugh as you were on the phone getting to know the new ones. As I watched you get dressed to go see them, remembering how we used to get dressed together, with you always looking at me like I was the most beautiful woman you had ever seen. As I stayed home with our boys, you ran the streets searching for something that you were not getting from me. I tried to be a chameleon, to change shape to fit what you needed me to be. To be the friend that I once was when you were having problems with the most recent one. To maintain my parental role because it was the one role that you did not have the power to rip away from me. I wanted to remain a constant in your son's life even when I wanted to run away from you because he was mine too, and he deserved me, consistency. You deserved me but I could never get you to see that as you constantly condemned yourself as not being ready for someone like me. Maybe it was just me. Maybe you always knew I was forever and forever is what you were running from.

Patience is waiting 30 minutes to check on someone if they are running late for a date. It is not sitting on the bench while someone else goes to play all night and hoping when they get home, they have energy to play with you too. This is acceptance. You are using non-verbal communication to explain to them that this is alright with you. That it is acceptable and you will be here when they need you no matter what. No matter how many times they do not come back. Some, would mistakenly call this loyal, some would say I am ride or die for these actions. I don't want to die to ride with you. I want to ride with you until the wheels fall off and then change the wheels out together so we do not have to stop. What some call loyalty, I call hope. Hoping that I could show you better than tell you that I was gonna be there and you could trust me, that I was fighting for us. Unfortunately, I was fighting with no one else in the ring!

Make sure that you are in a relationship with another and not alone. If they have one foot out the door and you are trying to pull them back in, that can never work. You need both feet planted in order to have a strong foundation. Power stance. If people are asking you to let them go, even if it goes against all your senses, do it. They may be making a mistake but it is theirs to make. If you hold on too tight, suffocating them with all of the things that could be, and things do not work out, they will only harbor resentment toward you for making them go through it longer when they were done a while back. No one likes to feel as if time was wasted. Now the pain is tripled because the investment has doubled. It is not worth adding more pain for either of you. One dose of pain is enough and we do that to ourselves on accident so why purposely add more?

Before you step in that ring willing to throw down all you have for a person, make sure that they are present. Are they in the ring with you? Then make sure that you are happy. I know that I was not happy sitting home with the kids when I was missing you immensely wishing that I was with you and not against. I was unappreciated and turning into that not-so-married woman that felt like her partner didn't take her out or want her anymore. This is because they are no longer your partner. You are two separate entities and they are living a life outside of you and you are in denial about it. You do not want it to be over so you cling to each and every last thread you can find until it snaps and you are thrown to the ground in defeat. You chose this route and it is painful so next time choose another. Learn the lessons that are presented.

You have the power to choose... Take those last few threads and tie them in a knot so that they are stronger for the next person. Feel the hurt, pain and loss and pick yourself up remaining strong for what life will bring you next. Life will always show you worse after you believe that it cannot. Remember to zoom out! This is but a small speck in the story of your life and if you take a moment to zoom out allowing yourself to see the full picture, this one moment will seem so small. That is because it is.

IN THE RING

Valentine's Day! I have always been against people making big life moments happen on a holiday. You can never forget it as the holiday will always come around and remind you. Then I did it to myself. Hahaha! We were going on a trip for the weekend and things were finally on pace for us. We covered all the big conversations and we had made it through, together. In the days leading up to the trip, I was standing in stores shopping for engagement rings. I had made up my mind and there is no changing the mind of a lion. Know that. There is no backing out once the decision is made.

The family was ecstatic and beyond ready to see this happen. I was nervous even then as I never planned on getting married at all, let alone being the one to ask the question. I was not sure that you would say yes but I was sure that I wanted you to. After finding the perfect ring, I thought I would be sick but I was eerily calm. When I held it in my hand, it just felt right. All nervousness went away and I was ready. I knew that I wanted to do something to show you exactly how I felt for you and all the progress that we had made. There was no bigger gesture than this as anyone who knows me knows I am not the woman that lays her heart out on a gold platter for anyone to possibly set on fire and then stomp out said fire. For you, I did it all!

We were in the hotel in Oregon celebrating Valentine's Day weekend. On bended knee, my hands shaking, I pledged to love you forever. I will never forget the initial shock on your face as your eyes bounced between mine and the ring I held in my hand. I explained how much you meant to me and that I did not want to go another day without you knowing that I was all in. We had been through so much together and we made it, somehow still together. We could make it through anything as long as we had each other. It was the only thing I could think of to show you how I felt. In that moment, I knew that I wanted nothing more in the world than you for you to say yes. At the end of my spiel, you looked at me with your nose slightly red and tears streaming down your face and simply said, "YES! Yes of course I would love for you to be my wife. I love you so much!" We cried together and I shakily got the ring on your finger. It was the happiest I could have ever been. We told our boys when we got back and they were ecstatic telling us it was about time, and it was our time…For a while…

I spent some time for the first time actually envisioning marriage. I was not one of those little girls that sat fantasizing of a white dress and flowers. It was all new to me and I was beginning to understand the high that others would speak of. Visualize the dress that would spark your eyes to tear up at the sight, the people who would be standing next to us emotional and excited. Choosing the song that would soundtrack the happiest day of my life. I was definitely in awe at momentum of the trance I was in. It is a huge ask to trust another with your heart, your every day for the rest of this life. I never thought that I could put so much trust into anyone else as I had not quite learned to put it into myself. Here I was in utter disbelief while synchronously methodical.

The security of knowing that there was at least one other human being on this planet who actually knew the real you, the strengths and the faults and still chose you. We all want to be chosen, don't we? What we tend to neglect is the fact that we were never taught to choose ourselves first. This is a lesson most of us learn much later in life and is a huge step in the personal growth that will increase your self-awareness. This usually happens as you are in the orbit of a significant other or spouse causing confusion for them. Remain transparent in your explanations. There will be changes and though we are taught early on that change is a negative thing, we must deprogram this thought process.

What we need to pay attention to when committing to another is that as the many other options become available, will they still choose you? In these days of complete overindulgence, can we hold on to the sacredness of what love truly is meant to be?

Bittersweet Anniversary

On this day I took my heart and gave it to you

Promises and future plans were agreed to

Cloud nine couldn't touch us as the tears fell in Oregon

Of all joy and trust, needed a siphon

As the moment passed and you grew distant from me

I could feel what was coming but prayed intuition fail me

You ran...full speed...all acceleration

And I broke, fell ill from the fluctuation

Took time and grew like a weed from the separation

Yet our hearts remain tucked away just where we left them

Regardless of whom else creeps through

No exceptions to the simple rule

You were created for me and I for you

We may never make it to that promised place

Still who we are cannot be replaced

And I can only pray we stay in this space

Where we love like us, slow and hard, vicious but soft

Tentative but stimulating, rough and raw

Bonnie & Clyde, no Vaseline

It will always be an anniversary to me

Though bittersweet

FOUNDATION

Friends for so long, friends so oblivious. We were such a tight knitted group of friends for a long time. I can remember the mutuals telling us that there was something between us. At times even accusing us of hiding some clandestine affair instead of letting them in on it. We vehemently denied all charges as they were wrong and we truly were just great friends. In hindsight, I realize that the connectivity was there long before either of us was even considering acknowledging it. Were we hesitant to risk the friendship or were we just so caught up in the number of relationships that we were in and out of? The relationships that we helped each other through. The break-ups that we drank about on your back porch until the early hours of the morning.

I can remember, it was one of these long talks when we started to discuss what we were really looking for. What we wanted and the things that were important to us. It became apparent that we had so many similar desires in a relationship. We were so used to the background noise. The barbeques, the smells of food on the grill, the Phase 10 shit-talking, the music, and sometimes the drama that surrounded us when we all got together with our plus ones who didn't understand that we were gonna have one another's back before anything else. When the noises faded and it was just you and me, I believe that we may have fallen back then at least to some degree. We began to protect each other viciously when people would hurt us.

Many nights in the club, far too many drinks and much laughter and fun. As the years flew by and relationships came and went and our children became family.

We were solid in our friendship and slowly changing. Something happened and that protective side of you kicked in. I was in a volatile relationship that only you were aware of and I struggled to be with a Jekyll & Hyde personality. One who was so fun to the outside party, everyone loved this person but they were different person behind closed doors: A severe alcoholic that I loved and wanted to help in any way that I could. We both had that tendency to attract those that we thought we could help. The ones that could love hard but hate harder. No one would believe that this same person that seemed to be so happy, was verbally abusive and violent when they seemed to love me so much. We could all be out at a park, having a blast, smiling and laughing, while I was watching how many drinks they would have and dreading what would happen when we made it back home. I noticed you watching more intently our interactions. You began to consistently check in to see to see if I was alright.

You began to protect me on a heart level as you noticed the changes that were taking place in this turbulent relationship. I had an especially rough night after a barbecue when the alcohol had taken over. I was done when the next morning, I was having a hard time getting this person to realize what they had done the night prior. Of course it was all my fault and I should have left them alone and if they had no recollection of the events, it didn't matter what had transpired. Instead, I should have left them to their devices and definitely not given them the bathroom trash can to throw up in instead of the carpet in my apartment. As that same trash can flew past my head, I knew that I wanted out. From there I was again wrong when explaining that I had gone to seek advice from a friend. Talking to anyone about our business accelerated things from bad to worse. This was it for me and for you as well. I decided to opt out of that relationship. They were not happy and refusing to leave when you and another friend came and helped get this person out of the apartment. I knew that this would bring about more trouble but it was worth it to me to end it. It was unhealthy and I had to learn that you cannot help those that do not want it.

The kiss

The first time freedom for each of us fell at the same time, there was a magnetic force that came into play with this rare occurrence. We decided to meet up and go get drinks at our favorite bar. I met you at your house and we headed out. I was so excited to see what the night would bring since we were always in a big group of friends when we were out. Instantly, we were in our own world. I failed to see anyone else in that bar that night. This never changed with us. We danced, we drank and we fell into the vibe that we would become known for. Afterward, as we sat in your car talking as we often had before, your eyes fell on my lips and you told me you wanted to kiss me so bad. I said "why don't you?"

When our lips met, I forgot it all. I was transported to a new place and time and I had never felt anything near the static that you brought to me. My body was on fire and I felt like I could kiss you forever. When your hand cupped my face, it felt like you were claiming me as all yours and no one else's. I had no objections. This! This is what people long for. It was honestly something that I hadn't believed in previously and still wouldn't had I not experienced it for myself. I would tell everyone who argued that they were just feeling the alcohol or something. That experience is something that has left me wanting and expecting. I wanted to feel something close to this again and expected that I would someday. These are the moments that lead us to compare. To test drive people and see if they can measure up to what we had before. They won't and unfortunately, they shouldn't.

That next morning, we were on the phone and I asked if you were alright after what had happened as I was looking out my blinds to see what the weather looked like. You said you were and the next line that came from your lips sent me swinging. You said, "We would be so good together." It stopped me in my tracks and I chuckled nervously but tried to play it cool. I asked, "Why do you say that?"

"Cause we would, think about it."

I did think about it. A lot. Too much even. The seed was planted and damn if it didn't grow as big as an oak tree.

One night, we were locked tight in my apartment still worried that the ex that didn't want to be an ex would show up. We had set all kinds of traps to alert us if anyone were to try to enter the apartment. Even though we were treading in new territory, it was a rush of need that caused us to remain there. Together. You held me on the couch as I sat in your lap and the tiny touches and exploration of each other was all-consuming, intense to say the least.

Always for me, I felt that the people you were with were not enough for you in that I wanted to see them truly appreciate you. I remember thinking this is insane. What are we doing with these people who cannot see us for who we are and do not care to because they have every intention of molding us to fit into their ideals.

There was one barbecue in my apartment that was a night of drinks, phase 10, and drunken jenga. Jenga leading to a bit of drama when people were kissing those that they were not with and all the insecurities that people tried to hide bubbled to the surface along with the alcohol. I recall many ridiculous arguments we would drink about later. You spending $2 on a soda and your partner wanted to make sure that we knew we had to give it back to you. It was hilarious because always in the circle, we would get things and the next time someone would balance it out by doing the same. There were those insecurities about you and me and our chemistry that at the time, we were not privy to. Not yet.

For some reason, people think that they can be, produce, and create the change that they want to see in another person. You cannot and will not change anyone. You are not the exception to any rule. It is harsh but it is real. We can only change ourselves therefore others can only do the same. This is something else that is not your job and you cannot sustain a relationship when you put all of your energy into wishing and hoping that they change for you. Why? Why do you want someone to change for you? The change will only be temporary and at some point they will fall back into what is second nature for them no matter what "work" you feel like you have put into it. Weren't they good enough to lead you to your current status? Why do you want to change them now? Again, I have to remind you that is not love. When you love someone, you do not want to change them, only to watch them grow and change on their own with you next to them. Be present to witness the changes but not be the reason for them. When people attempt to change "for" someone else, it is nothing more than a mask that they put on simply to placate said person. It will surely fade and they will fall into old habits fairly quickly as pretending gets hard to do.

Idle Hearts? Why have we never heard about this? At least I never did. I feel that this should be a developmental conversation subject. Are idle hearts the same as idle hands? We have all been warned about the hands but never the heart. I wonder why that is. The heart is a muscle and we work it each and every day without thought and without regard for all it does for us. Sounds eerily familiar to how we treat those we are with, huh?

We are idle creatures, spending most of our time in this position in one manner or another. Idle hands, idle hearts, and idle minds can all become instruments of destructive imagination. We know what happens when the hands are idle, people often find themselves doing things with them that they should not so suffice it to say that when the heart is idle, we may love who or what we should not. An idle heart can lead us to entertain avenues that would hold no interest for us otherwise. When we find ourselves bored we tend to do things simply to take up time, filling permanent positions with temporary things and at times this extends to temporary people. The fillers. We use them to fill the holes we have in our lives when what we should learn how to do is to allow the holes to be empty. They are cracks in our interpretation of ourselves that we feel make our imperfections known to the rest of the world when really, we are the only one to know that they are there. The truth of the matter is that the imperfection of your cracks are beautiful and allow your light to shine from the inside. If you fill these cracks with fillers and vices, you are dimming that light and no one can see it shining.

EMOTION INVASION

There was a point in our relationship where a sadness came over me. I no longer felt that you were interested in me but instead interested in anything but. I had become so dependent on the amazing feeling that you had always given me that without it, I was trapped in a sad state. I could no longer see myself the same. The natural confidence that I had was gone. Having been prone to depression since I was young, it wasn't long before that feeling, too had taken over. I was operating on autopilot day by day but could not feel as alive as I was used to. I began to feel like I was only happy with myself when I was not in your presence. You, the person who had always brought me joy and made me feel invincible. I struggled even with the simplest things, getting dressed, being active, it all seemed so much harder to accomplish the more time went by. What was an even harder thing to grasp is that I would be away from you and I would become myself again. The confidence would return and the feeling of worth would also reappear. Others would still SEE me and it felt so good to know that she was still in there somewhere. With you, I felt like I was not enough so I silenced her while trying to become who I thought you wanted me to be. Reminder: I had no clue as to who that was and could not have succeeded no matter what I tried to do as I did not know the true objective.

No one prepares us for these things. We are thrown into life with little to no knowledge of how to navigate these immense feelings and moods so we learn as we go and usually leave turmoil in the wake of it all. The fix for this is simple. Have the conversations surrounding emotional navigation. If people can learn how to deal with these things in a healthy manner, they will less likely seek an alternate route. This is especially true of children, they are sponges for all we teach them. Ensure that they know it is okay to feel and to express. Conversations are slim these days and this is where the change needs to happen. We must discuss to deprogram.

This was a rough spot for the both of us. Where I was in these feelings on my end, you were definitely not attracted to the decline of my self-esteem and failed to see the correlation in your treatment of me. Though I was previously unaware of this dependency, I had started to assume your perception of me and made it my own. These were words never spoken and more so what I thought was going on in your mind based on the way I was feeling. We like to say that others make us feel a certain kinda way but how much of this is our own mind monsters playing games with us? WE create a lot of doubts on our own without even knowing it. By the time we figure it out, it is too late. At this point we have created something bigger than ourselves and it has taken over the common sense side of our minds and we are inhabited by something foreign to our regular. I was left as a shell of myself in the house that was supposed to be my home. I was angry, disappointed, but most of all sad! It felt like you were already gone and there was nothing that I could do about it.

Do not let people tell you that anger is not okay. You are allowed to be angry at any given moment for any given reason as long as you are angry based on facts and not fiction. Facts: I was cheated on repeatedly by you. As a master of rationalization, you made sure, at least some of the time when the forethought allowed, that we were temporarily on a break prior to your indiscretions. You rationalize your actions which is a clear indication that what you were doing felt wrong at some point. I was disrespected in many forms of the word on a number of occasions, I bared witness to the stomach churning conversations you had with the newest pussy of interest. Yes, we are not talking about PEOPLE of interest. This was about pussy. This was about being in the company of people that do not come with the attachments, responsibilities, obligations, or explanations. No judgement cause that is what you wanted and or needed at the time. Unfortunately for me, you also needed to be alone to go through these motions. This left me feeling like a huge burden to you but I still never once doubted that you loved me. Never. Yes, I know that I sound like an idiot for admitting these things but we have all been there. The love was never lost and I could always see it and feel it. Love makes you endure things that you would never think you would. It was not a question of the love, which has always been there. This was about communication and acceptance, these being the things that we were each lacking.

There is a freedom in not feeling as if you have to answer to anyone. I get it. I hate to answer to people as well. I think it is the Leo in me. I often think why are you asking me questions? Dealing with someone who will allow you to hit it and pretend not to care about what you do when you are not with them makes sense. The women that will talk to you about how much you love me, the woman you still live with and parents your child, then still allow you to crawl into their bed and make them feel like they could be me. No one can be me for you, my spot will always be mine. The things that you grew to hate about these attachments and obligations are the same things that you miss when you are with others that do not have these qualities. You would set these make believe boundaries as a rationalization for what you were doing. How you would do X things with them and then Y things with me. How they knew how you felt about me so it was all good. How you had no intention of having sex with random women but there was a "connection" so it was to be forgiven.

We are connectors by nature. We are the people that others migrate to for guidance. We can create connection in any situation if we choose to and disconnection as well if it is deemed necessary. What you were really doing was letting them all know that you had someone in your life dumb enough to stick around through all of the bullshit you pulled and that there was no need to respect that relationship because you didn't. People treat your relationships the way that you do. You set the bar, the boundaries and the allowances of others as to how you treat the one you are with is their indication in how to do so. If you disrespect the relationship that you are in by seeking the attention of others, you are using non-verbal communication to let them know that they should not respect it either. So no matter how many times you'd tell people how much you loved me, your actions told another version of the story.

I can remember even trying to help you navigate through the women when they would begin to get too attached, when they wanted you to parent their children, to be in relationships, to fall in love, when you were done with them for one reason or another. There was so much anger and hurt inside me but I stood still through that storm. I was pissed that I was home with the kids every night while you were playing house with someone else's child after numerous conversations about why you did not want any more children. I could not understand the dynamics that you set yourself up for. I began to see that you were manipulating each situation. You made sure that every one of them came with a very specific flaw that would later use as a strategy for an exit plan. You carried this out flawlessly when they got too close or asked for too much. Again I am not judging as I think that we have all been in a situation where we planned the reason for leaving prematurely. I was the best "friend" I could be and tried to give you unbiased advice cause at that point, I was there more for your son than for you and I was losing respect for you at a rapid rate. I was beginning to feel resentment and that was something new to me. I did not like this at all. This skewed my vision of you and I was not okay with it. I feel as if it allowed some of the outside opinions to creep into my head and set up shop there. All of the negative words and energy fused into my head and that nagging thought that I should have listened to them a long time ago. That you were never going to be faithful and that I could do better. I saw you as better up until this point and when I could no longer see that person, I knew it was time to let it go. I had lost you and this battle that I was fighting against no opponent. Just myself.

You do not want to feel as if you HAVE to answer to your partner. What you should aspire to is that you, of your own volition, want to make sure that they do not worry, therefore you want to keep them posted. You want to feel as if they should be involved in every part of your life as they, too, should be a huge part of your life. A huge PART! Not your whole life. When you choose to bring others into your life, it can be difficult to allow inclusivity at one hundred percent. There are things you will want to keep all to yourself and this is okay. It is possible to compartmentalize your life this way but know that it will become harder as things progress and at some point the lines of all compartments will blur. This is not a loss of freedom but more a gain of trust between the two. You have to keep the pieces that make up your center. This was a big lesson for me. Learning that no matter how hard you love a person, they cannot be the center of it all. You have to be the center for yourself, they are welcome to orbit your center as long as you remain there.

This is the trick y'all... grab a highlighter or somethin'!

How do you get through the pain of loss, through heartbreak, through the feelings that take over? When the sense of loss is so great that you are having a hard time functioning? Identify the things that this person is doing for you or bringing to your life which you are not doing or bringing for yourself. Then, learn how to do these things for yourself and do them often. This will train you to understand that the things that you think you need from someone else, can be attained by you and you alone. You cannot relinquish all of your safety and security to another. You must hold on to these things and make sure that you can first take care of it on your own. From there, you can invite others to join you in that security and they are welcome to contribute but never to take over.

When you find yourself looking to someone else to validate you, it is time to take a step back and do a self-check. You are responsible for you and your children, no one else. Not your mama, not your daddy or all of the issues we carry from them. At some point you have to bag all that shit up and decide what you are going to do with it. Are you going to allow it to hinder your growth or are you going to work it out and flourish? Women have to stop dulling our shine for the sake of others. We are brainwashed from a very young age not to outshine others. Let's break this cycle.

We are taught to laugh at jokes that are not funny to appease a man's monstrous ego. Dress a certain way so that men will notice you but not too much because that could lead to trouble. Allow a man to fix things so they feel useful, speak in a feminine matter and don't cuss like a sailor. Wear heels and skirts so you look like a lady. Have children but keep your body the same as it was before them. All of these things get embedded in the brains of young women everywhere who are then later berated for bending to the whim of a man or woman when they have been programmed to do so. Only you can deprogram these detrimental thoughts and practices. Remember that you must discuss to deprogram. That is the first step in any healing process. Release.

Do not dull your shine, find someone that will polish it for you and add more sunshine to each day that you have here.

I can remember when I moved to another state in an attempt to strengthen the relationship between my son and his father. After being told that the reasons for the strain was due to the distance, I took it upon myself to do this. It was there that I celebrated my 30th birthday. Something happens at 30. Something beautiful where as a woman, you have grown into yourself and begin to pull the weeds in the garden of your life. People start to fade away and your circle reduces in size just as your confidence increases. This was true for me in a big way also. One evening after taking my son out to dinner, he says to me, "Mom, I think we can go home now." When I asked him why, he simply stated, "The relationship between me and my dad is where it is gonna be." It was that simple statement that set things in motion for me. Through my child, I learned that some relationships just are what they are. They reach a peak and there is nowhere else to go and you begin to allow that to be okay. As sad as I was for my son, he was okay with it so I needed to be also. It was a last ditch attempt at allowing absence to no longer be the excuse that I heard. Today, he is a young adult and that relationship is between them but he has never lost love so for that, I am grateful. It is truly inspiring that children can be so mindful as to how to navigate through such important relationships without having the experience at hand to draw from. They are incredibly honest and I think as we become adults we learn how to filter that honesty. This can be detrimental as we move through the lives of others. That is why it is so essential that we allow honesty in our relationships and friendships as well because matters of the heart is how we direct ourselves.

You and I had been in contact throughout this whole experience, some bad and some good, but still consistent. When I made it back, again, not for the first time, we were falling into the rabbit hole that is us.

It starts with nights of just sleeping together in the bed. Sometimes it was you cooking a delicious dinner and conversation that led to cuddling and getting well rested for the next day. I found myself in this position often and longed for the rest that came with your embrace. You would think after all that we had been through that the safety would have escaped it. That I would no longer feel this sense of security with you, let alone want to be in your arms. Oftentimes I would find myself leaving the bed of another to come to you and somehow it never felt wrong. Never gave it a second thought because you fed me in multiple ways no matter how short the periods of time spent. It is like an addiction to be stimulated in ways that are not sexual. To be touched in places most do not reach. It can be all consuming if you do not pay attention and catch it before it is too late.

I wonder now if I was doing to others as had been done to me. Was I putting them in the same position that I was unhappily in? We do that, don't we? In full transparency, I have to admit that yes, I think that I am guilty of this. That there are painful things that we go through and carry on with us no matter how unhealthy. We then project these feelings and situations onto others without realizing it. I was leaving them to spend time elsewhere and I can remember feeling so low when I was in this same position. Are we testing them then to see if they will do as we did? Will they stay or go? Will they be as hurt as we were? Were we weak to put up with all that we did if they walk away? If they stay, do they love us as we had loved? Does it prove anything at all? We become intrigued to figure out the reactions of another specifically to relate it to our own. You cannot get to know yourself while focused on another. You have to own your shit! Analyze your actions and reactions without conducting personal experiments with others, they deserve more respect than that. It can be hard to see these things happening in the moment so I urge you to check in with yourself often and see what your true intentions are.

Though I had no ill intentions, I caused pain to another as I selfishly made my choice to come to you. I did this repetitively and most likely would still. For this reason alone, I know that it was the wrong time to bring someone else into my shit. It had to be dealt with. I do not want to be in this position nor do I want to use another in this way. It is a confusing position as the high of being wanted or needed by someone you crave is enough to continue the behavior. The reality that they will put you down again to continue where they left off just before they picked you back up is a low that you hate to stomach. All the while you could have stayed in the warm bed where you left the third party who is trying to love you in the ways that you are loving the other. Who is this scenario fair to?

Absolutely no one.

It can be difficult to notice when you are bookmarking for another and there are many versions of relationships that can land in this category. Be it a family member that is an alcoholic who you are consistently helping to clean up the damage they cause or to hide the evidence. This can hinder any growth or acceptance that you could be helping them with. It could be a friend who has had a failed relationship and does not want to enter the dating world again. You fill the space and time for them in this instance. Yes you are a remarkable friend but could possibly be hindering any progress they could be making also. This could lead to a disastrous id circumstances change and your time is limited, changing this dynamic as they have not taken the time to heal and emerge unafraid. You are allowing others to set expectations for you and boundaries that are nonexistent. Bookmarks should show you where you are in order to move forward in the story. Nothing more and nothing less.

The problem for me was that I was becoming just a placeholder of sorts for you. When you needed a break from the current one you were with or just someone to talk to about the consistent incompatibility that you were dealing with, it was always me. You would call and I would come braced with the information that I knew you well enough to know that this was your way of saying that you missed me. You needed me to tell you if it was you or them and call you on your shit when need be. You hated that when we were together, yet yearned for it once we were not. Funny how that happens so often. The same things that people fell in love with you for will be the same things that they have a problem with later. This stems from reception. It may be sexy when aimed at another but your partner may find it difficult to swallow when it comes in their direction.

Bookmark

Stick me there to hold your place

When I long to be the pages that you read

The chapters of false suspense, Surprise that you long to
know about

You fill your time while you put me to the side

Oftentimes you twirl me between your fingers

Or hold me when your current chapters are uninteresting

-Too much, Not enough

This is when you pick me up

We both know that I am the goldilocks

The perfect fit – just right

Those worn corners will never be as strong as me

There is so much history in "we"

Bookmark

Pick me up when the chapters start or stop

At times in between when you get tired of the princess

And realize that you need a queen

I am every chapter printed, every piece of paper, even

Each drop of ink for the script

I am the binding that holds it all together without trepidation

My voice is the completion of your mental stimulation

I became enthralled at the character you'd play for these other women. So far from the woman that I had come to know. I wonder how much of the real you they ever got to see. I am sure that there were glimpses into her on occasion. We struggle to hold onto a front for too long, no matter the circumstances. When I say that we are connectors by nature, I mean this is ingrained in our personalities. We can connect so easily to others whether that be through conversation, music, passions, or sex. For us, entering into a sexual relationship is a risk. Attempting to find someone that can maturely venture into this and leave behind any emotional attachment is an unfair ask. We are attentive and we are givers, we are passionate and we are lovers. This will always lead to an emotional whirlwind for those that we share intimacy with. To even sit back and hear some of the things that were going on with you and others, I could understand why these women would fall into feelings with you. There is no warning strong enough to ward it off. You were repeating this cycle of looking for something light that would not bring the added stress of worrying about someone else's emotions.

People will tell you that they are looking for the same thing and then find themselves confused as to how they ended up in love. It is too late then and they now have expectations that you had not signed up for. I do not think there was ever an intention to hurt anyone that you were involved with, simply that you were naive enough to believe it could have ended any other way. This is an outside perception and I am not even sure if the presentations given to me were truthful or if you chose to edit and omit for the sake of my feelings?

Just remember that you have to be respectful to yourself and what you need in order to allow yourself to move in any direction. Otherwise you are walking with a flashlight rather than the sun. I find it hilarious how humans think that they can add any limitations to the measurements of pain they can cause another. Manipulating words in a false hope to lessen the pain that you cause another. I have to tell you that this helps no one. Both parties are then at a disadvantage. One now having to remember the stories told for future conversations and the other who does not have the proper information to make an educated decision as to which direction they want to proceed.

I think my curiosity was piqued as to how they could not see through it. Maybe they did not want to as that would mean the truth would be present. The truth that I now see. When there is something real and tangible between two people, there is no way to fight it off or avoid it. We have pushed each other far away. We have gone years without a call, text, or a sighting. Yet, when we do end up in the presence of each other, it is undeniable. Immediately going to us having consistent conversation that stimulates the parts of our brains untouched by others whom may have been in the picture in between time. There is this need for more. The dinners, the sleeping. This unforgiving pull of magnetism that brings us here, locks us in and we begin to wonder why we are not back to us entirely if it feels this way and we have not been able to find anything even close to it.

We would soon fall into the sexual part for which the magic has brought many tears of joy and (X)stasy to the pillow..

Special thanks to all who helped throughout this journey.

Phyllis, Jeremiah, Janay, and all of my wonderful tribe who read through the pages with nothing but positive words and feedback to convey.

If this book has helped you in any way, please pass on these lessons.

Together, we heal!